3/01

23.⁹⁰

CLOCKS AND RHYTHMS

ALVIN SILVERSTEIN • VIRGINIA SILVERSTEIN • LAURA SILVERSTEIN NUNN

TWENTY-FIRST CENTURY BOOKS

BROOKFIELD, CONNECTICUT

Cover photograph courtesy of Tony Stone Images (© Brian Stablyk)

Photographs courtesy of Photo Researchers, Inc.: pp. 4 (© Rafael Macia), 9 (© Jany Sauvanet), 12 (© John Sanford/Science Photo Library), 25 (© Ted Spagna/Science Source), 47 (© Blair Seitz), 53 (© Will & Deni McIntyre); Visuals Unlimited: pp. 10 (© Arthur Gurmankin), 16 (© Tim Hauf), 18 (© Nancy P. Alexander), 21 (© Barry Slaven), 32 (© D. W. Gotshall), 36 (© Joe McDonald), 39 (© Tom J. Ulrich), 41 (© D. Cavagnaro); Animals, Animals/Earth Scenes: pp. 14 (© Breck P. Kent, both), 23 (© Patti Murray), 42 (© Rich Reid); TK: p. 17; Werner Forman Archive, Biblioteca Universitaria, Bologna, Italy/Art Resource, NY: p. 19; The Granger Collection, New York: p. 33; UPI/Corbis-Bettmann: p. 46; NASA: p. 51; Liaison International: p. 55 (© Le Corre-Ribeiro)

Library of Congress Cataloging-in-Publication Data

Silverstein, Alvin.
Clocks and rhythms / Alvin and Virginia Silverstein, and Laura Silverstein Nunn.
p. cm. — (Science Concepts)
Includes bibliographical references.
Summary: Discusses the concepts of time and biology cycles, including the phases of the moon, the internal clocks of plants and animals, seasonal rhythms, and the aging process.

ISBN 0-7613-3224-3 (lib. bdg.)
1. Biological rhythms—Juvenile literature. [1. Biological rhythms.] I. Silverstein, Virginia B. II. Nunn, Laura Silverstein. III. Title. IV. Series: Silverstein, Alvin. Science concepts.

QH527.S45 1999   98-26058
571.7'7—dc21   CIP
                                                                              AC

Published by Twenty-First Century Books
A Division of The Millbrook Press
2 Old New Milford Rd.
Brookfield, Connecticut 06804

CONTENTS

Early sunsets during the winter make rush-hour traffic in New York City more difficult.

ONE

WHAT TIME IS IT?

Every morning you probably wake up to the sound of your alarm clock ringing. Feeling drowsy, you wonder, *What time is it?* Then you look at the clock and shut off the alarm. You mustn't be late for school, so you rush to get dressed and eat breakfast. When you get to school, you may keep an eye on the clock to see when classes will end. Finally, the school bell rings to let you know it is time to go home.

In today's busy world we look at clocks all the time. They control our lives. They tell us when to get up, when to eat, when to work, when to play, and when to sleep. Clocks are so much a part of our lives that we would hardly know what to do without them.

If you didn't look at a watch or a clock, would you be able to tell what time it is? Would you know when it is time to wake up? To eat lunch? To go to bed? If you looked out a window, you might find some clues to what time it is. If the sun is shining brightly right overhead, it must be noon. A dark sky filled with twinkling stars means it is nighttime. How close to the "correct" time would your guesses be?

✦ SECRET CLOCKS ✦

Do you need a clock to tell you when to do the things you do? Many scientists think not. They say that, although you may not be conscious of it, you have some built-in **biological clocks** constantly ticking inside your body. Your biological clocks tell you when to feel hungry, sleepy, or wide awake. Scientists who study these biological clocks are called **chronobiologists**. Chronobiologists have discovered that our bodies have **biological rhythms** that send messages to our brains to tell us when it is time to do things, such as sleeping or waking.

Animals and even plants are also able to "tell time" without looking at a clock. They, too, have inner rhythms that regulate their daily activities. Some animals, for example, are active during the day and sleep at night, just as we do. Others are active at night and sleep the day away in a burrow or another safe place. Plants may lift up their leaves and open their flowers during the daytime and close them up tight at night.

✦ BUILT-IN CALENDARS ✦

All living things have built-in calendars. We have not only daily rhythms but monthly and seasonal rhythms, too. Many living organisms are strongly influenced by the moon's near-monthly cycle. The moon takes about 29 1/2 days to revolve around the earth. Some animals engage in mating rituals that depend on the moon's cycle. For instance, the silvery grunion fish in California come together to spawn (breed) shortly after a full moon or a new moon. Women's reproductive systems follow a cycle similar to the moon's revolution in which **hormones**—chemicals that help to control the body's activities—are secreted at certain times of the month.

Many living things are strongly influenced by the rhythm of the seasons. For instance, woodchucks, ground squirrels, and bears need to eat large amounts of food during the summer and fall months to prepare for the cold winter, when they will enter a sleeplike state called **hibernation**. They draw on these extra reserves of body fat during hibernation so they can survive through the winter months when little or no food is available. Some birds, such as geese, **migrate** twice a year. They fly south for the winter, to warm places where food is plentiful, then return in the spring to their northern homes to bear and raise their young. Many animals also mate according to the seasons, often in the spring and summer months. Plants are likewise affected by the changing seasons. In the fall, the leaves on certain trees die and fall to the ground. In the spring, flowers start to bloom and the grass turns lush green.

Like plants and like other animals, humans are affected by seasonal rhythms. For instance, people's moods often change according to the seasons. People are generally happier in the summer than in the winter, because summer days are longer, providing more light.

The artificial clocks and calendars that set the pace for our lives today do not always agree with our inner clocks and rhythms and those of the planet we live on. To get along in the modern world, we make compromises. We often ignore our inner body rhythms, staying up to watch a late TV show, waking to an alarm clock when we'd rather keep on sleeping, and eating meals on a schedule rather than when we are hungry. In today's world we use clocks to keep everyone running on roughly the same time. If people were allowed to live their lives according to their own individual inner clocks, it would be a very disorganized and confusing society. We do not always realize the price we may pay to live "out of synch" with our natural clocks and rhythms. Chronobiologists believe that learning more about nature's rhythms may help us learn to get along better with our inner clocks and live healthier and more productive lives.

TWO

RHYTHMS OF OUR PLANET

Where do our biological clocks come from? These inner clocks have been shaped by the forces of nature to fit into the rhythms of our planet.

Millions of years ago the first signs of life appeared on the earth. These organisms existed on a planet that already had daily, seasonal, and **lunar** (moon) cycles. All living things developed inner cycles as a result of adapting to a world that itself is cycling. People evolved from organisms that had adapted to the constantly changing environment in which they lived.

✦ DAILY RHYTHMS ✦

Imagine a ball with a pin stuck through the middle. The ball can turn, or **rotate**, on the pin. Our earth is very much like that, with the pin, or **axis**, an imaginary line running through the globe from the North Pole to the South Pole. The earth is constantly moving. It takes 24 hours for the earth to rotate on its axis. As one side turns toward the sun, the sun's rays fall upon it—and it has daylight. When that side of the earth turns away from the sun, the sun's rays are blocked and it is left in darkness.

Life that developed on earth had to adjust to these periods of daytime and nighttime. During the day, the sun's light is an important source of energy. Plants use the light energy to make food in a process called **photosynthesis**.

The light thus helps trees, grass, and other plants to grow and flourish. Some animals developed special sense organs (eyes) that could use sunlight to see things. These animals are active mostly during the daylight hours and rest during the dark nights. Some of them feed on plants; some eat other animals, using the light to find and catch them. Some prey animals have survived by being active at twilight or at night, using the darkness to help them hide from predators. But predators have adapted, too. For instance, bats are active at night. A bat can locate its prey in the dark sky by making high-

Like this European wildcat, the house cat is equipped to hunt in the dead of night.

pitched squeaks, which bounce off objects and come back to the bat's ears. Through this process of **echolocation**, the bat uses the patterns of reflected sounds to find its way in the dark and locate its prey. Cats, too, developed special adaptations. In addition to their sharp hearing and keen sense of smell, they have eyes that can magnify the dimmest starlight or moonlight, which helps them to pounce on their prey at night.

The cycles of day and night have had a significant influence on the behaviors of humans as well as plants and animals. Until a few centuries ago people planned their activities entirely according to the hours of daylight and darkness. They were active during the daytime, but they rested at night. These daily rhythms worked well with the rhythms of the earth. In the summer, when days were longer and the weather was mild, people could put in long hours growing crops, tending animals, and doing other chores that required light to see. In the winter, when days were short and the weather was cold, people spent more time sleeping during the long, dark hours of night. This allowed them to conserve energy during the season when food was scarce.

Light is the most important external cue that influences our biological rhythms. Thomas Edison's invention of the electric light bulb in 1879 had a dramatic impact on people's inner rhythms. To a much greater extent than earlier light sources—candles or oil lamps, for example—the light bulb made it possible for people to stay active when it was dark outside.

✦ SEASONAL RHYTHMS ✦

The earth takes about 365 days to **revolve** around the sun. This makes up a single year. Over most of the earth, living things had to adapt to changing seasons throughout the year. Why do we have four seasons—spring, summer, autumn, and winter? Because the earth is tilted, different parts of the earth get different amounts of the sun's light and heat. Areas near the **equator**, the imaginary line that goes around the middle of the earth, receive the most direct sunlight. Areas near the poles get the least. Areas in between get different amounts of sun, depending on how far north or south of the equator they are.

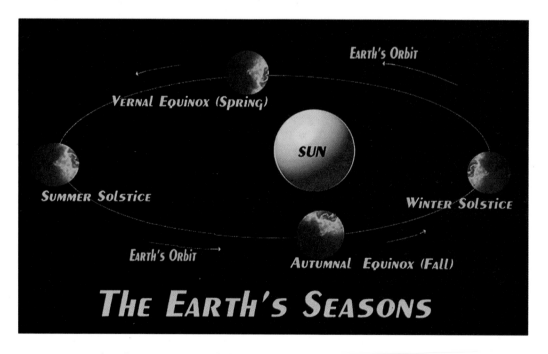

Day and night occur on earth because it turns on its axis. The seasons occur because the axis is tilted, so that different amounts of sunlight and heat hit different parts of the earth at different times.

North of the equator—in the Northern Hemisphere—summer begins on June 20 or 21, the summer **solstice**. The sun reaches its highest point (farthest north) in the sky. There are more hours of daylight than on any other date, making it the "longest day" of the year.

Autumn, or fall, begins on September 22 or 23, the autumnal **equinox**. At this time the sun appears directly above the equator. There are 12 hours of daylight and 12 hours of darkness.

Winter starts on December 21 or 22, the winter solstice. The sun reaches its lowest point (farthest south) in the sky. There are fewer hours of daylight than on any other date, making it the "shortest day" of the year.

Spring begins on March 20 or 21, the vernal equinox. The vernal equinox is similar to the autumnal equinox because the sun is located just above the equator and there are 12 hours of daylight and 12 hours of darkness.

South of the equator—in the Southern Hemisphere—the solstices and equinoxes occur on the same dates, but the seasons (spring and fall, winter and summer) are the reverse of those in the Northern Hemisphere.

The change in the seasons meant a change in the activities of many living things. For instance, certain animals learned to prepare for hibernation or migration during the winter. Those that did not get ready for the cold winter months ahead had less chance of surviving. Those that did survive passed on their adaptations to future generations. Certain trees and plants also go through a kind of hibernation, losing their leaves during the fall and winter. With the colder weather and the reduced hours of daylight, the energy needed to keep the leaves healthy and growing is greater than what they could produce by photosynthesis. The plants conserve energy by becoming **dormant** until springtime, when the leaves grow back and the flowers bloom as the daylight hours increase.

✦ MOON CYCLES ✦

Many living things also adopted biological rhythms that were similar to the cycles of the moon. Like the earth, the moon is always moving. It takes the moon about 27.3 days to travel around the earth. Meanwhile, it spins on its axis, so that the same side of the moon is always facing the earth. As the moon moves

The earth is the ball at the center. The outer ring shows a composite time-lapse image of the phases of the moon. Counterclockwise from the top: new moon (causing solar eclipse), waxing crescent, first quarter, waxing gibbous, full moon, waning gibbous, last quarter, and waning crescent. The inner ring is artwork, with the green portion (facing the earth) showing why these phases occur.

around the earth, its appearance goes through a series of changes because the sun lights up different parts of the moon's side that faces us. These changes are called the **phases of the moon**. The entire cycle takes about 29.5 days, because the earth is moving, too.

The moon goes through the following phases:

New Moon: When the moon is between the earth and the sun, the sun's light falls on the side that we cannot see, so the moon is completely dark as viewed from our planet.

Waxing Crescent Moon: When the moon starts to move away from its position between the sun and the earth, we can see part of the moon lit up as a crescent with pointy horns at the ends.

First Quarter (Half Moon): When the moon and the earth are the same distance from the sun, the right half of the moon appears to be lit up.

Waxing Gibbous Moon: The moon starts to look fuller and we can see more of its lighted side.

Full Moon (Second Quarter): We can see the entire lighted side of the moon, which appears to be a completely round bright disk in the sky.

Waning Gibbous Moon: The moon starts to move back toward the sun, making part of the moon begin to darken again.

Third Quarter (Half Moon): Like the first quarter, only half of the moon's lighted side can be seen, but now the left half is lit up.

Waning Crescent (Old Moon): Only a thin sliver of the moon can be seen from earth.

The moon's cycle is completed when it returns to the New Moon.

The moon has a powerful effect on the earth. Its gravitational pull causes our oceans and certain rivers to rise and fall every day, producing **tides**. **Gravity** is a force that attracts objects to one another. Although the sun affects tides, too, the moon's effect is greater because it is so much closer—even though the sun's gravity is stronger. As the moon moves in its orbit around the earth, its gravitational attraction pulls the water, forming bulges (high tides)—one on the side of the earth facing the moon and the other on the opposite side.

In most places along shorelines, there are two high tides and two low tides each day. The water rises highest (and advances farthest onto the shores of the lands) when the shore is facing the moon. This is the first high tide. About six hours later, the water level reaches its lowest point and part of the shore is dry; this is the first low tide. The second high tide occurs when the shore is facing completely away from the moon. About six hours later, there is a second low tide.

> DID YOU KNOW?
>
> A second full moon in a calendar month is called a blue moon. It happens rarely, so the expression "once in a blue moon" means very seldom.

As the tides rise and then fall, the ocean waves carry along animals and plantlike organisms, which provide a wealth of food for the animals living along the shore. Millions and millions of years ago, some of the coastal animals developed cycles of activity taking advantage of the tide-borne bounty. Other animals developed mating rituals timed to the moon's monthly cycles. Scientists believe that animal life developed first in the water and later moved onto land. Perhaps that is why the mating of some land animals, as well as the water dwellers, seems to run on lunar time.

Low tide and high tide in Canada's Bay of Fundy shows the dramatic difference in water levels.

THREE

KEEPING TIME

For thousands of years people have been interested in the concept of time. The sun, the moon, planets, and stars have been important instruments for measuring the passage of time. Ancient people studied the movements of these heavenly bodies through the sky to determine the days, months, years, and seasons. The sun's daily movement across the sky indicated the **solar day**. The time it took for the earth to circle the sun marked the **solar year**. And the movement of the moon and its varying shape from new moon to new moon indicated a **lunar month**.

About 5,000 to 6,000 years ago, human societies were becoming more complex and more civilized. As they formed governments and formal religions, people realized they had to organize the measurement of time more efficiently. As a result, ancient civilizations in the Middle East and North Africa created clocks and calendars to keep track of the time.

✦ THE EARLIEST CLOCKS ✦

Several thousand years ago the shadow clock was the earliest device used for measuring time. When a stick was placed in the ground, the sun's bright light would make a shadow on the ground. People could measure the changing shadow as the sun moved across the sky throughout the day. By 3500 B.C, the Egyptians improved this primitive shadow clock into a device called the **sun-**

dial. The shadow was the shortest when the sun reached its **zenith**, or the highest point in the sky. This marked the middle of the day—what we call noon. The shadow was longest soon after sunrise and right before sunset.

The Egyptians' concept of noon meant that the day could be broken up into two equal parts— forenoon (morning) and afternoon. Eventually, another ancient people, the Sumerians of Babylonia, who lived in the Tigris-Euphrates valley in what today is Iraq, divided the time of light into twelve equal parts. These divisions began at sunrise and ended at sunset, which is when the Sumerians' new day began.

A sundial—decorative and useful, if you know how to read one.

The sundial was a very useful time instrument, but it had some problems. It could not be used at night or when it was cloudy. In addition, the length of day would change throughout the year, which meant that the twelve parts of the day also changed. In summer the daylight lasts a long time, so the twelve parts go by very slowly. In winter the daylight is short, so the twelve parts go by very quickly. The length of the day also differs depending on the location—the latitude.

Eventually, other devices for measuring time were invented. For instance, the water clock keeps time by water running into a container at a constant rate. When the water level reaches each of a series of markings on the inner surface of the container, a set period of time has gone by. Water clocks made it possible to divide the day into equal parts that did not change in length with the time of year. They could be used to measure time

Did You Know?

The Babylonian number system was based on 12, rather than the multiples of 10 we use today. That is why a complete day is divided into 24 hours, each hour into 60 minutes, and each minute into 60 seconds—all able to be evenly divided by 12.

During the 1840s the idea of time zones was first introduced in England, Scotland, and Wales.

Cities in the United States had determined the time according to the position of the sun. By 1860, with trains capable of traveling long distances, cities started to adopt time zones. However, at one point, there were some 300 different time zones across the country, making keeping time very confusing. The number went down to 100 when railroad time zones were created. In 1883 the United States was divided into 4 time zones. The following year the International Meridian Conference in Washington, D.C., decided to apply these time zones all over the world. Today there are 24 standard time zones, although some countries or regions use their own local times.

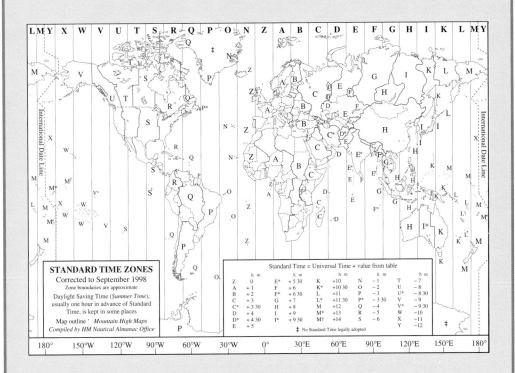

Because of political boundaries, time zones around the world have become more complicated than just counting off one hour for every 15° of longitude (360° that make up a circle, divided by 24 hours in a day).

Mechanical clocks of many kinds sit in the repair shop.

during both daytime and nighttime. The time units were named **hours**, from the Greek word for "time of day." Each cycle of daylight and darkness took a total of 24 hours.

Mechanical clocks like the ones we use today were not invented until about 600 years ago. These clocks could then measure the passage of time even more precisely, ticking off not only hours but also minutes and seconds.

✦ ANCIENT CALENDARS ✦

Clocks help us keep track of the time during a day—the hours, minutes, and seconds. But calendars keep track of time on a larger scale—days, weeks, months, and even years.

About 5000 B.C. the Sumerians made the earliest calendars. They based their calendar on 12 lunar months of 30 days each. But that came to only 360 days per year, and it takes the earth a little more than 365 days to travel around the sun. So they added an extra month every 4 years to keep their calendar "in line" with the seasons. The Sumerians later changed their calendars to alternating 29- and 30-day months to follow a 354-day lunar year. In this calendar, they had to add an extra month three times in an 8-year period. This Sumerian calendar had many inaccuracies and was very confusing.

About 4200 B.C. the Egyptians made the first calendar based completely on a solar year. They noticed that the "Dog Star" (Sirius, in the constellation Canis Major)—the brightest star in the sky as seen from the earth—was next to the sun at sunrise every 365 days. This happened about the same time as the annual flood of the Nile River. The Egyptians used this knowledge to devise a 365-day calendar, made up of 12 months, with 30 days in each month and an extra 5 days added at the end. About 238 B.C. they added an extra day every 4 years, similar to today's leap year.

Clocks and calendars are a convenient way to keep track of time. Most of us use these devices to organize our lives. As a result, our biological rhythms are forced to follow these artificial timekeepers.

"Magical" calendar created by the Aztecs of ancient Mexico.

✦ FOUR ✦

DAILY
RHYTHMS

Do you ever wake up in the morning right before your alarm clock is about to ring? You lie in bed just watching the clock, waiting for it to reach the "right" time. You may often find yourself waking up at the same time during the week. You may even wake up early on the weekends even though you do not have to get up at any specific time. How can your body know what time it is?

You probably do not realize this, but from the moment you wake up in the morning, your body goes through a series of mental and physical changes to get you ready for the day's activities. These changes occur during a 24-hour period in regular cycles, or rhythms, called **circadian rhythms**. (*Circadian* comes from a Latin phrase meaning "about a day.") These circadian rhythms are controlled by a biological clock in your body that regulates various rhythms, including wake–sleep cycles.

✦ PLANTS SLEEP, TOO ✦

More than 2,000 years ago, ancient Greek scientists had already observed and commented on daily rhythms, not only in humans but in various animals and even in plants. Hippocrates, a Greek physician, noticed that his patients' symptoms seemed to vary in a regular pattern each day. Herophilus of Alexandria, another Greek physician, found that the pulse rate also changes in a daily

The eighteenth-century Swedish scientist Carl Linnaeus, who devised a system for classifying plants and animals that is still used today, was fascinated by the daily movements of plants. He noticed that plants that bloom in the same season may open and close their flowers at different times of the day. The African marigold, for instance, opens at 7 A.M., the Star-of-Bethlehem at 11 A.M., the passionflower at noon, and the evening primrose at 6 P.M. After Linnaeus published his list of flowers that opened or closed at each hour of the day, people in Europe used it to plant flower beds in the shape of a clock. At certain seasons of the year, they could look out the window and tell what time it was by observing the flowers.

Flower bed in the shape of a clock in present-day Christchurch, New Zealand.

rhythm. The fact that certain plants opened and closed their leaves at regular times each day was so well known in ancient times that there was a myth to explain it: The plants were showing their love for the sun god, Helios.

Some of the first scientific experiments on daily rhythms were conducted on the "sleep movements" of plants. Everyone assumed that the opening and closing of the plant leaves was a response to the presence or absence of sunlight. In 1729 a French astronomer, Jean Jacques d'Ortous de Mairan, decided to test this "obvious" assumption. He placed a plant in a dark closet and peeked in at it at various times during the day and night. Even though the plant was in total darkness, it still opened its leaves during the daytime and closed them at night. The plant seemed to have some internal clock that kept the time even without the external cue of sunlight. De Mairan had some ideas for further experiments but was too busy with his work in astronomy to follow them up.

In 1758 another French scientist, Henri-Louis Duhamel, repeated de Mairan's experiment, with some extra precautions to make sure no light leaked in to provide a time cue. He put his plants in a trunk, covered with blankets, in a closet in an underground wine cellar. Duhamel got the same results. He also established that the plants' rhythms were not being influenced by temperature changes, since the temperature down in the cool cellar stayed constant.

In 1832 Augustin de Candolle, a botanist, made a further discovery about plants' internal clocks in a series of experiments on mimosas. Whether in darkness or in constant light (provided by lamps), de Candolle's plants continued to open and close their leaves in a regular rhythm—but the cycle repeated itself each 22 hours, not the 24 hours of our planet's rotation! This was the first demonstration of "**free-running**," the tendency of organisms (both plants and animals) to exhibit circadian rhythms even in the absence of external cues. These cycles are about a day long, but not usually *exactly* 24 hours. They are determined by heredity and vary not only from one species to another but even among individuals of the same species. Biological rhythms generally range from 20 to 28 hours.

When de Candolle exposed his free-running plants to natural light, they soon adjusted their cycles to a 24-hour period. He then demonstrated that they could respond to external cues by reversing the day-night cycle: Plants exposed to artificial light at night and kept in darkness during the day adapted to this new schedule within a few days, opening their leaves at night (when they were in the light) and closing them during the day (when they were in the dark).

If plants have regular daily cycles, what about the animals that depend on them? For instance, bees gather nectar and pollen from flowers. It would be most efficient for the bees to visit particular types of flowers when their petals are open. Sure enough, researchers have discovered that bees have internal clocks that help to time their rounds. In the early twentieth century one scientist noticed that a crowd of bees showed up regularly and buzzed around the jam and marmalade jars as his family ate breakfast on the porch of their sum-

*It's no coincidence that these two pollen-covered bumblebees are
feeding at the same time: Their biological clocks send
them to this flower when it is open to receive them.*

mer home. When the meal was moved indoors, the bees still showed up at
breakfast time and buzzed at the windows. Another researcher reported that
bees visited buckwheat fields only between 10 and 11 A.M.—the time of day
when the flowers secrete their nectar. In 1927 the German researcher Ingeborg
Beling trained bees to come to a feeding table for a meal of nectar. Then she
began putting the nectar out only between 4 and 6 P.M. Soon the bees were vis-
iting the feeding table only at those hours of the day. They continued to arrive
on schedule even when the scientist stopped putting out bowls of nectar. In
another experiment, the researcher was able to train bees to come for food the
same time each day even though they were kept at the bottom of a salt mine,
600 feet (183 m) underground, where they could not see the sun. However, she
was unsuccessful in attempts to train bees to look for food every 19 hours or
every 48 hours. Those times were too far from the bees' natural rhythm, which
turned out to be 23.4 hours.

In 1955 a French researcher, Max Renner, trained bees to feed between 8 and 10 P.M. in a room in Paris where lighting and temperature were carefully controlled to eliminate external cues. Then the researcher flew with his bees to New York, where a similar controlled room had been set up at the American Museum of Natural History. There was a five-hour time difference between New York and Paris at that time, and sure enough—promptly at 3 P.M. New York time (when it was 8 P.M. in Paris) the trained bees went out looking for food.

Experiments on internal clocks have been conducted on numerous other animal species. Charles Darwin, for instance, who is now famous for developing the theory of evolution, published a best-selling book on his studies of earthworms and observed that they stayed underground during the daytime and came out only at night. In general, it has been found that **nocturnal** animals, which are active mainly during the nighttime, have natural cycles that are less than 24 hours long. **Diurnal** animals (including humans), active mainly during the daylight hours, typically have circadian rhythms that are longer than 24 hours.

✦ OUR BODY RHYTHMS ✦

Shortly before you wake up in the morning, hormones flow from your glands into your bloodstream to get you ready for your daily activities. As you get ready for school—brush your teeth, take a shower, get dressed, and eat breakfast—your heartbeat speeds up and your breathing becomes more intense.

Throughout the day your body goes through other changes. By late afternoon your body temperature has gradually increased about 1°F since morning. Your blood pressure, which is lowest during the early morning, fluctuates during the day until it reaches its peak by early evening.

Later at night, after the day's activities, you start to feel tired. While you are sleeping, your body goes through even more changes. Deep within your brain a structure called the **pineal gland** secretes a chemical called **melatonin** that flows into your brain to make you feel sleepy. The highest levels of melatonin occur about

> DID YOU KNOW?
>
> According to a recent poll, the average American adult gets 6 hours and 53 minutes of sleep each night during the week and 7 hours and 31 minutes a night on the weekends. Fifty-one percent of men and 42 percent of women say they would go to bed earlier if it were not for TV and the Internet; thirty-seven percent of the people say they are sleepy during the day.

2 A.M., rising to about four to six times greater than during the day. If you woke up during this time of night, when the melatonin is at its peak, it would be very difficult to do even simple tasks. The increased levels of melatonin cloud your concentration and judgment. In fact, the secretion of melatonin is high during the early morning hours even when a person is awake, and it is no coincidence that the numbers of industrial and traffic accidents are greatly increased at this time. There is a sixteenfold increase in one-vehicle collisions in the early morning hours, for example.

Sleep also brings other changing circadian rhythms. While your body is at rest, there is a decrease in respiration, heart rate, and blood pressure. The urinary system is also less active while you sleep. That, in addition to not drinking, is why you can go through 8 hours at night without going to the bathroom. The overall metabolic rate—the rate of the chemical reactions that go on in the body—also drops. The secretion of growth hormone, however, increases. About half the total day's amount of growth hormone is released during the first few

Changing positions and locations in bed is normal for this man
and his cat as they share part of a night's sleep.

hours of sleep, and most of the growth and repair of body tissues occurs during sleep. By morning the cycle starts all over again.

Circadian rhythms can be set off by external cues, such as the sun rising in the morning, and the darkness of the night. These external cues can be powerful motivators, but they can be controlled by pulling down shades or by turning the lights on. Our bodies may also respond to other cues, such as changes in temperature. But we can modify that as well by turning the heat on or cooling our rooms with air conditioning. Though external cues help to guide circadian rhythms, they are not really necessary. Circadian rhythms are automatic, occurring whether we want them to or not. The lack of external cues may adjust our circadian rhythms somewhat, but studies show that our bodies will continue to cycle with or without cues. Most people, if left without external cues, would follow a 25-hour cycle rather than the 24-hour one of the earth's rotation. In everyday life, however, we use our planet's cues to synchronize our clocks so we can fit smoothly into our world.

✦ TIMING IS EVERYTHING ✦

If you plan your activities according to your various circadian rhythms, you would be doing your body a huge favor. Timing is very important when it comes to inner rhythms. For instance, if you want to lose weight, the best time to eat a big meal is in the late morning, when your metabolism is at its peak. Most people in the United States eat their largest meal at dinnertime, which is really a bad time to eat such a big meal. By bedtime the heavy meal is still being

In 1938 U.S. sleep researcher Nathaniel Kleitman and a student spent two months in Mammoth Cave, Kentucky. The temperature was constant, and they could set the periods of light and darkness by turning electric lights on and off. First they tried to live on a 21-hour day. They adapted successfully and lived this way for a month. Then they tried stretching their day to 28 hours. The student adapted to this longer day, but Kleitman found that he could not. His body rhythms were out of synch with the external cues, and he felt ill and irritable.

Many other isolation experiments have been conducted since this first study. In one, for example, medical students from London spent a summer in Spitsbergen, Norway, where it is daylight all summer long. The students were given "cheating" wristwatches that were set to run fast or slow. These time cues had one group living on a 21-hour day, while another was on a 28-hour day. The students were able to adjust their sleep-wake cycles to the apparent time, but some of their body rhythms stayed closer to a 24-hour period.

In a study in 1962, a group of researchers lived for months in caves without any external cues. Their bodies continued to cycle, but their rhythms became "free-running." Soon they were following a two-day schedule without even realizing it. An Italian subject of another study, living in isolation, found that her perception of time became distorted, and her body rhythms shifted several times.

digested. During sleep metabolism slows down; less of the food is "burned" for energy, and more is stored away as fat.

Exercising also depends on the time of day. People have the greatest strength by late afternoon. That is the best time to do sit-ups or push-ups because your lungs are at their greatest capacity. Nearly all the track-and-field records in the past century were set in events in the late afternoon.

Doctors often schedule diagnostic tests for patients during the mornings. But that may not be the best time for all tests. For instance, the early morning is actually the worst time to test for allergies. In fact, patients who were given scratch tests at different times of the day developed the most redness and rash around 11 P.M. This is not a very convenient time for doctors to check your reaction. Actually, your skin can be a hundred times more sensitive to allergic reactions around midnight than it is earlier in the day. If you are allergic to dust particles in your room, or outdoor pollen is in the air, you may wake up sneezing in the morning. You might notice that your allergies seem to settle down as you go through your day. Then, by evening, the runny eyes and stuffy nose may start up again.

Doctors have learned from chronobiology that the health of their patients depends on the time of day they receive their medication. For instance, when patients were given the same dose of a drug for lowering high blood pressure at different times of the day, the drug was more effective at 6 P.M. and at midnight than at any other times.

Timing may be everything in chemotherapy (drug) treatment for cancer patients. An experiment on mice that had leukemia, a form of blood cancer, showed that these animals could be either killed or "cured," depending on the time of day that they received the same amount of chemotherapy. When the drug was given at 2 A.M., 96 out of 100 mice died; when the same dose was given at 8 A.M. or at 5 P.M., only 4 out of 100 died. Treating a human cancer patient with chemotherapy at the best time of day may be a matter of life or death. Doctors also need to know the patient's circadian rhythms of cancer cell division. Chemotherapy is most effective when the cancer cells are dividing at their peak.

DEVELOPING BIOLOGICAL CLOCKS

Our biological clocks start ticking before we are born. When babies are born, their bodies already have temperature cycles. By about seven months of age, babies have developed rhythms of sleep. But these cycles are "free-running," because they are not yet linked to the world's external cues. Babies' urinary rhythms take longer to develop, which is why they need to wear diapers. The high activity level of ten-year-old children throws off their circadian rhythms. Adolescence is a time of "growth spurts" and major development, requiring more sleeping time. Yet teenagers often tend to skimp on sleep, getting less than they really need, and their circadian rhythms are also irregular. Our bodies generally settle down to a regular 24-hour day by the late twenties or early thirties. Elderly people have a tendency to have more sleep problems than other age groups, however, and their energy levels are greatly reduced, which can mess up their circadian rhythms.

Timing may also be very important for certain types of surgery. The common practice of scheduling surgery in the early morning may be harmful to patients whose body systems are still at their sleeptime lows. And good timing may involve not only time of day but time of month. The success rate of breast cancer surgery has been closely linked to a woman's menstrual cycle. Studies have shown that women who had surgery in the middle of their monthly cycle, near ovulation, when the amount of the hormone estrogen in their bodies is at its highest level, had fewer recurrences of the cancer than women who had surgery during the time of menstruation.

In the plant and animal world good timing is also very important. For instance, if a firefly flashes its light at the wrong time of the day, chances are that a mate will not respond. Flowers must keep their petals open during the day when bees are active and can pollinate them. Nocturnal predators (animals that hunt at night) usually have special adaptations that allow them to hunt prey at night so they can take them by surprise.

✦ WHERE IS THE BIOLOGICAL CLOCK? ✦

Our body time is controlled by the **suprachiasmatic nucleus (SCN)**, a cluster of cells found within the **hypothalamus**, a portion of the brain about the size of a cherry. This control center can be influenced by light, acting as an external cue. How does light produce effects deep within the brain? Light rays enter the eyes and strike the retina, a layer of sensitive cells at the back of the eyeball. Messages from these cells are sent along nerve fibers of the optic nerve to a vision center in the brain that interprets the messages into meaningful images. Meanwhile, a branch from the optic nerve carries light messages to the pineal gland, buried deep within the brain. This is the gland that secretes melatonin, a hormone that makes us sleepy, and also affects other body rhythms. Nerve fibers connect the pineal gland to the SCN in the hypothalamus, thus delivering the messages from the eyes. The SCN is also linked to many different parts of the body. For instance, if light enters the eyes, messages travel to the hypothalamus, then to the SCN. From there, the SCN is able to send information about time to the rest of the body.

In some experiments, when researchers electrically stimulated the SCN of an animal, its circadian rhythms shifted and went through a free-running period. When the animal's SCN was destroyed, its rhythms of drinking and activity were eliminated. It took several months for the cycles to disappear completely, as other controls continued to operate for a while.

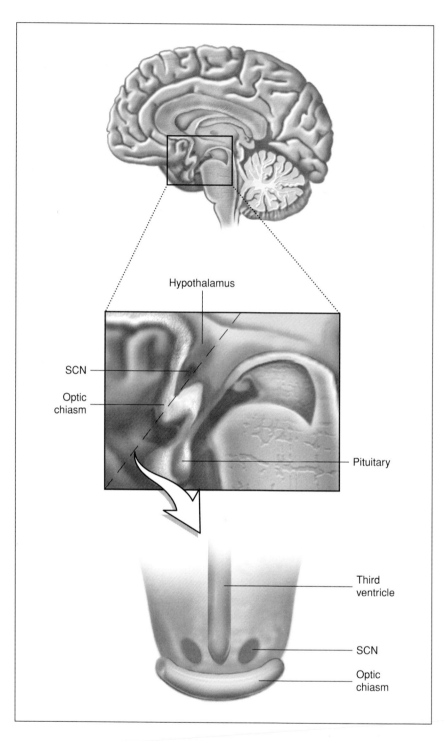

*Our biological clocks are controlled by the SCN,
located deep inside the brain.*

Biological rhythms that occur more often than once a day are called **ultradian rhythms** ("ultra" means going beyond). There are short ultradian rhythms, such as your brain waves, which respond in rhythms of a fraction of a second; your heart beats every second; and you breathe every six seconds. Other ultradian rhythms are longer—cycles of an hour and a half (90 minutes) that regulate periods of rest and activity. For instance, you start to lose concentration and begin to daydream about every 90 minutes. Similarly, when you sleep, you dream about every 90 minutes or so. People also tend to get hungry in 90-minute cycles.

✦ FIVE ✦

MONTHLY RHYTHMS

Many animals that live by the sea seem to know just when the tides will come in. In fact, their daily activities are often perfectly timed to the tides, which are, in turn, governed by the movements of the moon. For instance, sea anemones—flowerlike creatures with long tentacles—are anchored to the ocean floor. Since they cannot move, they need to keep track of the tides, which mark their feeding time. When the water is calm, sea anemones look like little blobs, their tentacles falling limp on the ocean bottom. But when the tide rises, their tentacles flow with the rising water, catching tiny bits of food floating or swimming nearby.

Other sea animals such as oysters, clams, and mussels also time their activities to the tides. For instance, oysters open their shells at high tide, to filter out bits of food from the rising water. As the tide goes out, the oysters'

The sea anemone may not get around, but it can spot a tasty meal. As a starfish wanders by, the anemone's tentacles seize it.

shells shut tight, protecting them from drying out when they are exposed to the sun and air. In an experiment, a marine biologist took some oysters in a tank of water from a fishery in Connecticut to a laboratory in Illinois. These oysters continued to open and close their shells in perfect rhythms with the tides on the east coast, even though their home waters were 1,000 miles (1,600 km) away, in a different time zone. After two weeks in their new home, the oysters had reset their clocks to the moon's cycle by Illinois time.

Humans have monthly cycles according to the moon's phases just like animals do. The moon's gravitational pull on the earth may have a powerful effect on a person's mind and body.

✦ MOON MADNESS ✦

For centuries, people have linked all sorts of strange behavior to the moon. Some ancient people believed that the moon had some kind of mystical powers. They thought that the moon was responsible for bizarre happenings, from making women pregnant to driving people crazy. In fact, the word *lunatic* comes from the Latin word *luna*, meaning "moon."

Today, people still credit the moon, particularly a full moon, for many strange things—from the birth of babies to murder and chaos. For instance, some nurses have observed that more babies seem to be born on the night of a full moon than any other night.

During a full moon some people have a ten-

This seventeenth-century engraving depicts the belief of the time that the moon has a bizarre effect on these women's lives.

dency to get a bit restless and possibly a bit out of control. In fact, many psychiatric hospitals have records that show a sharp increase in admissions. Bartenders say people tend to drink more and are more likely to get into fights. Police officers have reported that there appears to be a dramatic increase in "crazy" people running the streets.

There is no conclusive evidence that shows a connection between the moon and madness. But there will always be people who believe in the power of the moon.

✦ THAT TIME OF MONTH ✦

The idea that the moon may have powerful effects on people does not seem far-fetched to chronobiologists. They point to the most obvious lunar rhythm: a woman's menstrual cycle. This cycle averages 29.5 days—the length of the lunar cycle—though individual menstrual cycles can vary as much as 25 percent. In fact, the word **menses**, the technical term for the periodic flow of menstrual blood, actually means "lunar month."

SYNCHRONIZED FRIENDS

Female roommates often have their menstrual cycles around the same time. This happens because during "that time of month," women give off certain chemicals called **pheromones**. These pheromones act as external cues that regulate their monthly cycles.

Biological rhythms often overlap one another, so the menstrual cycle also produces other changing patterns. A woman's body defenses become weaker during menstruation than at other times in the month. For instance, a woman is about 30 percent more likely to have allergic reactions during this time than in the middle of the cycle. Skin problems, such as acne, are a common complaint during this time of month. Other physical ailments may also occur: tonsillitis, hives, herpes sores, ulcer attacks, and especially headaches. Nearly two thirds of women who suffer from headaches say that they occur on menstrual and premenstrual days. Asthma attacks are also more likely to occur during or shortly before menstruation—up to 75 percent during these times. At the middle of the month, women are more likely to catch colds or the flu—as many as 77 percent caught colds when exposed during this time of the month.

Women may also go on an emotional roller coaster just before or during menstruation. Some symptoms of the **premenstrual syndrome (PMS)** include anger, irritability, emotional instability, and weeping. Scientists have found that the levels of three important hormones—the sex hormones estrogen and progesterone, as well as aldosterone, a hormone of the adrenal gland that helps to regulate the balance of body fluids—peak right before menstruation. These hormones can have significant effects on a woman's body and brain.

Men actually have monthly rhythms, too. There is not as much research on the monthly rhythms of men as of women, however. As early as the 1930s, an industrial psychologist named Dr. Rexford B. Hersey studied men in their workplace to see if they displayed a pattern of behavior similar to the emotional cycles of women. Hersey found that men also had fairly regular mood swings. Many actually followed a rhythm of about 28 days. During part of the cycle, the men would be in a cheerful mood, joking with their co-workers and feeling full of energy. By about two weeks after the high point of the cycle, the men would be reaching an emotional low, feeling moody and lethargic and avoiding social interactions. At the low point of the cycle, some of the men had trouble sleeping, lost weight, and showed other physical symptoms.

Dr. Christian Hamburger of Denmark continued Hersey's work, trying to determine if male sex hormones, like those of females, caused them a pattern of changing moods. Dr. Hamburger took samples of his own urine each day for a period of almost two decades. An analysis of these samples showed that there was indeed a definite monthly rhythm. Another chronobiologist, Bob Sothern, at the University of Minnesota, kept records of his mental and physical state several times a day for more than twenty years. He found monthly variations in the amount of air he could hold in his lungs, the strength with which his hands could grip objects, and the growth rate of his beard.

✦ BREEDING BY THE SEA ✦

Samoan palolo worms carry out a breeding ritual in the form of an extraordinary dance. This ritual is clearly linked to the moon's monthly cycle, as it is perfectly timed to the waning moon in the months of October or November. People who live in Samoa and the Fiji islands, in the South Pacific, know the timing of this spectacular event and gather to watch it.

The palolo worms spend most of the year down among the coral reefs in the waters where they look for food. To prepare for their annual breeding ritual, they grow a number of extra, foot-long segments on the end of their bodies, which contain their sex cells, eggs and sperm. When the moon is at its waning

Fire in the Sky

It was a moonless night on October 11, 1492, as explorer Christopher Columbus sailed on the *Santa Maria* toward what he thought was the Far East. He was actually 7,000 miles from his destination and instead witnessed an interesting event. At 10 o'clock Columbus noticed a light on the horizon and figured it was a sign of land ahead. The light flickered like a candle, and Columbus was not sure what he had seen. It was only later that another sailor on the sister ship *Pinta* sighted land.

Five hundred years passed before anyone could explain what Christopher Columbus had actually seen: the mating rituals of Atlantic fireworms, marine worms that live in waters around the Bahamas and reproduce according to the moon's cycle. During this breeding ritual, the fireworms release glowing streams of eggs into the water once every month, just one hour before moonrise on the night before the new moon.

Great numbers of horseshoe crabs mate at the same time along a Cape May, New Jersey, beach.

phase in October or November, the worms come up to the surface in swarms to reproduce. The long segments break off and churn around in the water, making the water look like boiling soup.

The islanders quickly scoop up some of the worms' pieces and take them home to cook. The rest of the segments in the water burst, releasing the worms' eggs and sperm. The sperm join with the eggs and fertilize them, starting off the lives of a new generation of worms.

Many other sea animals also have their mating habits timed to the phases of the moon. Many bottom-dwelling fish come up to spawn, or breed, at set times. The silvery California grunion, for example, spawn from March to August right after either a new or a full moon.

✦ SIX ✦

SEASONAL RHYTHMS

If you walk outside, can you tell what season it is simply by looking at your surroundings? In the earth's temperate regions, there is usually something distinct about each season—spring, summer, fall, or winter—that lets you know the time of year. For instance, we know it's spring when we hear the first birds chirping, the early flowers start to bloom, the grass turns green, the trees grow new leaves, and the outdoor temperatures start to warm up slightly. Summer is a time of hot temperatures, swarms of insects feeding on crops (and on people), trees full of leaves, and dried yellow-brown grass. During the autumn, the leaves on the trees turn different colors—yellow, orange, red, brown—and start to fall to the ground, and the temperatures start to get cool. Winter is a hard season to miss: the temperatures are very cold; it may snow; and only a few hardy birds or squirrels can be found outside.

Why do we have seasons? As the earth moves around the sun, we receive different amounts of light at different times of the year. For instance, during our spring and summer months, the sun shines most directly on the part of the earth where we live, giving us the greatest amount of sunlight. We get the least amount of sunlight during the fall and winter months. The changing of the seasons, that is, the amount of sunlight, has a powerful effect on our planet. In fact, almost all living things have biological rhythms that are timed perfectly with the seasons.

Most animals can tell what season it is without calendars. The amount of daylight is their cue. The daylight hours decrease during the fall months. In temperate climates, this is a clear indication to many animals that winter is coming and it is time to prepare for the cold months ahead. Animals that cannot survive the cold temperatures or face a lack of food sources during the winter get ready for hibernation or migration.

Hibernating animals such as ground squirrels, bears, and woodchucks spend the autumn months, and perhaps much of the summer as well, filling up on food so they can live on their fat reserves through the winter. Hibernation is a method of survival for these animals. They generally remain in a deep, sleeplike state, while their bodies undergo some major changes to conserve energy: Their body temperature falls, often to within a few degrees of their environment. Their heartbeat slows, as does their breathing. It is extremely difficult to wake them up—they look almost dead. Months pass in this hibernating state, until the animals' biological clocks tell them it is time to wake up.

Many species of birds migrate during the autumn months to prepare for winter. These birds fly to areas farther south, where the temperatures are warmer and the food is more plentiful. The decreasing day length cues them to fatten up, storing energy reserves for the strenuous flight. Studies show that migrating birds often rely on the position of the sun and the stars to find their destinations. But these navigational tools also depend on biological clocks because the position of the sun and stars changes over time. Inner rhythms help to guide the migrating birds to where they need to go.

Animals that do not try to escape the winter have their own ways of coping with

A black bear survives the winter in a rocky den by hibernating—slowing down its bodily functions so that it uses little energy.

bitter-cold temperatures. During the fall, when the days are getting shorter, these animals grow thick winter fur. In the springtime, they go through a process of **molting**, a seasonal shedding of the heavy fur, allowing them to cope with the hotter summer temperatures.

Many different kinds of animals have a molting season, in which they shed their fur, skin, or feathers and grow a new body covering. For instance, birds molt at least once a year. Feathers wear out, just as you wear out your clothes. In many species, the new feathers gradually replace the old ones, without hampering the birds' ability to fly. Ducks and geese, however, lose all their feathers at once, so they cannot fly for a while.

They spend a lot of time in the water while their new feathers are growing. Other animals that molt include reptiles, such as snakes and lizards, which shed their skins; and shellfish, such as lobsters and crabs, which shed their outer coverings (shells) and replace them with new ones. Some animals even shed some body parts. Deer, for instance, shed their antlers and grow new ones.

✦ MATING SEASON ✦

Most animals have a mating season, but the particular time of the year varies. There are two main patterns in the timing of the mating season. "Short-day" animals breed either in the early spring or late fall, when there are fewer than 12 hours of daylight. Such animals include species with quite different habits. For instance, sheep, which feed on plants and live in herds, breed in the fall. Black-footed ferrets, predators that feed on prairie dogs and live alone, mate in the early spring. "Long-day" animals breed in the late spring or summer, when there are more than 12 hours of daylight. Such animals include raccoons and cottontail rabbits. In general, mating seasons are timed to take advantage of the periods of the year when food and living conditions are favorable for raising the young.

Domestic cats and dogs do not have a special mating season. But the females do have breeding cycles in which fertile periods—when they are "in heat"—alternate with times when mating does not occur. Over many generations of breeding by humans, these animals have lost their seasonal timing and can reproduce all year round.

A male Indian peacock courts a female by displaying his amazing tail.

Some animals adapt in unusual ways to the seasons of their home. Grizzly bears mate in the late spring or early summer, and it takes about two months for the babies to develop—but grizzly bear cubs are not born until January! After a female bear has mated, the development of the fertilized eggs stops temporarily. The mother spends the summer and fall eating and fattening up. When winter comes, she finds a cozy den to hibernate. That is when her babies develop, and they are born while she is still fast asleep. The reserves of fat that the mother bear stored for the winter provide for her own needs and for the milk she produces for her cubs. By the time the cubs are ready to venture outside, it is spring.

✦ SEASON OF MISERY ✦

Like the rest of the animal world, people cannot escape the effects of daylight on biological rhythms. Many people feel more tired and less energetic during the short days of winter than on the long days of summer. But for some people,

Seasons in northern Alaska and Canada are very different from other parts of the United States and Canada because of their far-northern latitudes. For as much as three months in the summertime, there is no night. Like Norway and Sweden on the other side of the world, northern Alaska in the summer is the "land of the midnight sun." In the winter, though, there is no sunlight at all from as long as late November to late January. The weather is very severe, too, with low temperatures and high winds that keep people indoors most of the time. Some of the Inuit who live in northern Alaska suffer from a kind of "madness" called Arctic hysteria each winter. The attacks usually last from a few hours to several days. Scientists have discovered that these Inuit lose large amounts of calcium in their urine during the winter. This mineral plays an important role in transmitting messages in the brain and nerves. The lack of calcium may be the cause of the temporary attacks of "madness."

*These canoers take advantage of the midnight sun
on Canada's Yukon River.*

these dark days plunge them into deep misery. These people have an illness called **seasonal affective disorder**, or **SAD**, which is a severe depression that occurs every year as a result of decreasing daylight. SAD affects as many as one in fifteen people. People with SAD behave normally throughout much of the year. But when the short days of winter come, they find it hard to get out of bed, go to work, eat, and basically function effectively in society. SAD patients may require medication to get back to normal. Some SAD patients are treated with light therapy: bright, artificial light is used to make the days seem longer.

When the sun shines down on the earth, the curved surface and the tilt of the axis make different places receive different amounts of light. Those closest to the equator get the greatest amount of light. Those farther away get the least amount of light. Therefore, the number of SAD sufferers differs depending on where they live. For instance, in the United States, people in Florida have less than a 2 percent risk of developing SAD. In Maryland, however, which is 1,000 miles (1,600 km) farther north, the rate more than triples. In New York, there is an 8 percent risk of getting SAD. But in Fairbanks, Alaska, as many as 25 percent of the population shows some signs of SAD. Thus, in the Northern Hemisphere, the farther north you live, the greater your chances of suffering from SAD. (The reverse is true south of the equator.)

SEVEN

RESETTING THE CLOCK

Do you feel more tired on Mondays than any other day of the week? You, like many other people who work or go to school Monday to Friday, are very familiar with the Monday blues. You may think it's because people do not want to go back to school or work. That may be true, but chronobiologists believe that we could very well blame our biological clocks. During the week, our circadian rhythms run on a fairly consistent and predictable schedule. But on the weekend, people tend to follow their own personal body clocks, going to sleep a little later than usual and waking up a little later. The usual weekday sleep–wake pattern is thrown off. Getting the "Monday blues" is actually your body's response to having to reset your biological clock.

✦ TIME TRAVEL ✦

We know that Thomas Edison's invention of the light bulb had a major influence on biological rhythms by shifting people's wake–sleep cycle. Another invention has had a powerful effect on the rhythms of a part of the population—travelers. That invention is the airplane, specifically the jet plane. Jets have made it possible to travel at speeds of more than 500 miles (800 km) per hour, allowing you to fly from New York to California in about 6 hours. In doing so, you cross the boundaries of three time zones—California's time is 3 hours earlier than New

York's. If you left New York at 3 P.M., you would arrive in California about 9 P.M. New York time—almost bedtime. But in California the time is only 6 P.M. Californians are ready to sit down to dinner, while you are already starting to feel sleepy. Such shifts in the external cues caused by the rapid flights over long distances can disrupt the body's rhythms, resulting in a condition called **jet lag**. This malady literally did not exist before the twentieth century. Older forms of transportation took days to move from one time zone to another, allowing the traveler to adjust gradually.

Can you imagine how you would feel if you traveled from New York to Australia? Sydney, Australia, is 15 hours later than New York's time. When it is noon Monday in New York, it is 3 A.M. on Tuesday in Australia!

Many experiments have been conducted to show the effects of jet lag. In one experiment, the same effects were produced without any actual travel, by using controlled lighting to simulate the time zone change. At the start of the experiment, the subjects were monitored to establish their normal temperatures, skills, moods, and sleep patterns. After about a week, the researchers moved up the schedule of lighting and meals, so that the external cues made it seem to be five to eight hours earlier. After another week, the subjects clearly showed signs that are associated with jet lag. Their biological cycles, such as the changes in body temperature and levels of various body chemicals, seemed to have lost their synchronization. They were irritable, less motivated, and suffering from a variety of physical and mental symptoms often associated with jet lag. The physical symptoms included sleep difficulty, hazy vision, headaches, sore throats, upset stomachs, aches and pains, poor coordination, and a decline of strength and reaction time. Mental symptoms included difficulty concentrating, memorizing, or learning; a constant weariness; and mental confusion. The fact that all these changes were due to the change in time cues rather than any distance traveled is further supported by frequent observations that long flights north–south or south–north do not produce any symptoms of jet lag.

> DID YOU KNOW?
>
> About one in twelve travelers claim they have never had jet lag. Of the other eleven, five or six have had severe jet lag. Some people may need only a day to adjust to time travel; others may take several days. The speed of recovery depends on the individual, the number of time zones crossed, and the direction of the time change.

In the early 1930s pilot Wiley Post became the world's first, and possibly even worst, case of jet lag when he set out to fly his airplane around the world in eight days.

After traveling about 15,500 miles (25,000 km), Wiley Post stopped at an airport to fuel up. Post was greeted by news reporters, cheering crowds, and a marching band to celebrate his newsworthy trip. Soon after Post got into his plane and took off, he turned his plane around and came right back. He was so tired that he had forgotten to fill up his fuel tank! At another stop, while Post was speaking to a reporter, he fell asleep right in the middle of answering questions. Other times he couldn't tell if he was on the ground or in the air. Post said he felt like he was flying his airplane even when he was sitting in the passenger seat of someone's car.

Wiley Post (center, without a jacket) and Harold Gatty certainly look the worse for wear after their 8-day, 16,000-mile (26,000-kilometer) plane trip around the world in 1931.

✦ SHIFTING TIME ✦

You probably imagine that most people in the working world have 9-to-5, 5-day, 40-hour-a-week jobs. But what about the people in the transportation industry—in airplanes, trains, and trucks? What about health-care workers, fire fighters and police officers, teachers who take home papers to grade, telephone operators, and people in the military? How about the people who work on the weekends and in the evening—restaurant and custodial workers, entertainers, and gas-station attendants? These people work in shifts around the clock so they can be there when we need them. What shift work does is make people ignore their inner cycles and follow the demands of the economy. As a result, working shifts makes people feel like they are walking around in a state of "shift lag," a condition very much like jet lag.

Many companies assume that shift work increases productivity. It seems to make sense—if there are people to work at different hours around the clock, then more work will get done, right? Well, it is not that simple. The

This surgeon is feeling the effects of too-long shifts at the hospital.

rhythms of the workforce may not agree with the rhythms of a person's body. When you go against your body's usual schedule, your physical and mental abilities suffer. For instance, the fluctuation of body temperature throughout the day may influence how able you are to function. In the morning your body temperature rises, and the ability to learn and absorb new information is the most effective between 9 and 11 A.M. By afternoon the body temperature falls and your mental sharpness goes on a steady decline. Fortunately, by late afternoon your temperature starts to rise again, peaking about 6:30 in the evening and letting you feel "smart" again. By midnight, however, your mental abilities start to decline again. Your energies are at their lowest point during the early-morning hours, when thinking clearly and even lifting things is a struggle. People who work the late night, or "graveyard," shift from 11 P.M. to 7 A.M., have to fight feelings of sleepiness. Since by nature people are active during the day and sleep at night, graveyard-shift workers are actually going against nature.

LONG DOCTORS' HOURS

The long hours of doctors in training is a major concern in health care today. Doctors need to be alert and well rested when they provide treatment for their patients. Studies have repeatedly shown that a lack of sleep results in poor job performance. In the case of a doctor's job, it can be the difference between life and death.

In one case, a young woman was admitted to the emergency room and died 8 hours later. The intern and resident who treated this woman had already been working for 18 hours. This case was brought to court, and the grand jury ruled that the number of consecutive hours that the resident and intern had been working did indeed contribute to the woman's death. Laws were passed to limit the hours in a row that medical residents are required to work, but many experts feel they are still too long.

Many people, especially those on late-night shifts, try to trick the body into staying awake by filling up on coffee. It contains caffeine, a powerful stimulant that helps the body to function against its natural urges. However, studies show that the most accidents that occur on a job happen during the late-night shift. In fact, some of the most serious accidents in the world's history occurred during the late shift. For instance, in 1979, at 4 A.M. some very tired late-night workers made a number of mistakes at the Three Mile Island nuclear power plant near Middletown, Pennsylvania. These mistakes turned into a public-safety hazard, allowing radiation to leak outside the nuclear power plant. About eight years later a worse disaster occurred at the Chernobyl nuclear power plant in Ukraine. In the early-morning hours, some very tired workers there made mistakes resulting in an explosion that spread radioactive contamination throughout the area and across borders into nearby countries.

Studies of workers during late shifts have shown that the number of mistakes increases sharply around midnight and continues to rise until 4 A.M. Then mistakes drop significantly until their shift ends around 7 A.M. People who change to different shifts from day to day or week to week are likely to have the greatest problems resetting their inner clocks.

✦ DAYLIGHT SAVINGS TIME ✦

Every year, we "spring forward" and "fall back" for Daylight Savings Time. These are the only times we get to change our clocks. Daylight Savings Time was first suggested in an essay by Benjamin Franklin in 1784. But it was not taken seriously until the early twentieth century, when, during World War I, it was seen as a way of increasing productivity. Turning the clock ahead an hour in spring and backward in fall went through several variations during the twentieth century. In 1986, the United States and Canada adopted our present schedule.

Daylight Savings Time is similar to hopping on a plane and crossing over one time zone. Like jet lag and shift lag, this semiannual clock-changing event also gives us a kind of time lag. Shifting our schedules one hour may not seem like a big change in our daily routine, but it does have a dramatic effect on our performance. Generally speaking, "losing" an hour seems to have a greater effect on us than "gaining" an hour. We tend to become more tired and less alert than usual. For instance, scientists have found that when we "lose" an hour during the spring, there is an 11 percent increase in traffic accidents. When we "gain" an hour during the fall, the increase is only 3.4 percent.

> **DID YOU KNOW?**
>
> We are more likely to get sick when our biological clocks are out of synch. Our bodies' defenses wear down and become weaker when our rhythms are not regular. We become more susceptible to colds or the flu, asthma attacks, headaches, and other ailments.

EIGHT

BIOLOGICAL CLOCKS AND THE FUTURE

Science-fiction writers have speculated on many different aspects of time and our inner clocks and rhythms, as they may affect us in the near and distant future. If our population continues to grow, for example, cities may become so crowded that people will have to share buildings and services more efficiently. One way to do this would be to increase the amount of shift work, so that people could use the same offices, factories, restaurants, and other facilities at different times of the day and night.

If the trend toward increasing shift work continues, more people will have health problems due to shifting body rhythms. Research on ways to adjust these rhythms may help to make life more bearable in such a future world. Some progress is already being made.

Studies of the pineal gland and its hormone melatonin, for example, have led to a way to treat insomnia and prevent jet lag. People with problems getting to sleep can help to regulate their biological clocks by taking a dose of melatonin an hour before bedtime. A person's natural melatonin production tends to decrease with age, so taking a supplement can be particularly helpful for older people, who often have sleep problems. This hormone has also been used to regulate the body rhythms of blind people, who cannot pick up the external time cues of changes in light. A number of studies have shown that people who reset their internal clocks by taking melatonin can fly across time zones without developing any symptoms of jet lag.

✦ SPACE TRAVEL ✦

When humans venture out into space, they lose the external time cues of their home planet. Astronauts in orbital flights around the earth are exposed to light–dark cycles lasting from 80 to 140 minutes, as the planet blocks out the sun's light for about 30 to 40 percent of the time in each revolution. The *Apollo* astronauts suffered from sleep disturbances, including **insomnia** (an inability to fall asleep, or to remain asleep for the normal time), poor-quality sleep, and even prolonged sleep for up to 12 hours at a time. These disruptions of their normal body rhythms could lead to lapses in alertness and poor work performance during routine and emergency tasks. Space-shuttle crews now train beforehand under controlled conditions of light, darkness, and activity to help them to adjust to the time schedule of their missions. During actual flights in deep space, voyagers can take their planet's rhythms along with them by rotating the spacecraft, opening

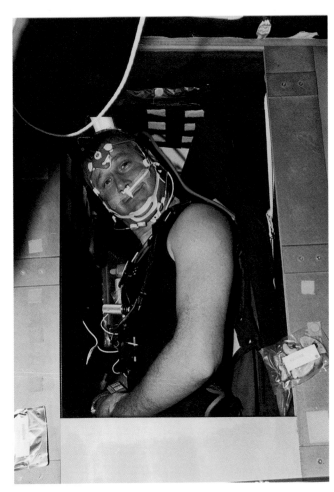

Jay C. Buckley, Jr., prepares for bedtime in his bunk aboard the Space Shuttle Columbia with equipment to monitor his sleep in ways similar to those of sleep labs on earth.

and closing shutters on windows, or turning lights on and off to establish the needed cycle of light and darkness.

If humans establish colonies on other worlds, they will be living under conditions quite different from those on Earth. The lengths of the day and the year would not be likely to match those of our home planet. In our own solar system, for example, Mars has a day length of 24 hours and 37 minutes—close to an Earth day—but it takes 687 days to make a full trip around the sun. Mercury, however, has a "year" of just 88 days but rotates much more slowly on its axis: Its "day" is 59 Earth days long—two thirds of the length of its year! Because of this slow rotation and the fact that it is not tilted on its axis as Earth is, Mercury has no seasons as we know them, and the sunlit side is burning hot (950°F, or 510°C), while the dark side stays freezing cold (−346°F, or −210°C). There are no tides or lunar rhythms on a planet like Mercury, either, since it has no moon. The tidal rhythms would also be quite different on planets that have more than one moon, or moons of a different size than ours. (Mars has two tiny moons, for example, while Jupiter has sixteen, one of them larger than Earth.) Would we be able to adapt to the rhythms of another planet, or would human settlers suffer from a constant "jet lag"? Probably most people would eventually synchronize their body rhythms to those of their new home, but some might have more difficulty. (Actually, some people never really manage to adapt to our own Earth's rhythms; their body clocks keep shifting later each day, and their various inner rhythms are "out of synch" with one another.)

✦ UP CLOSE AND PRACTICAL ✦

It's fun to speculate about far-out possibilities like establishing colonies on other planets, but chronobiologists are already pointing the way to some practical applications of biological clocks in the present and near future. The realization that temperature, blood pressure, heart rate, and other body processes show regular variations over the course of the day has led to more testing using 24-hour monitors that store a series of readings on a computer chip, instead of just taking a single measurement at one particular time. These results are providing insights that can be used for better diagnosis and treatment of medical problems.

In one study, for example, the temperature of the skin over a normal breast was found to show wider daily variations than the skin temperature over a breast with a cancerous tumor. In another study, women in Kyoto, Japan, who have a very low rate of breast cancer, showed greater seasonal and daily fluctuations of the amount of prolactin (a hormone that stimulates milk production and may be linked to breast cancer) in their blood than women in Minnesota,

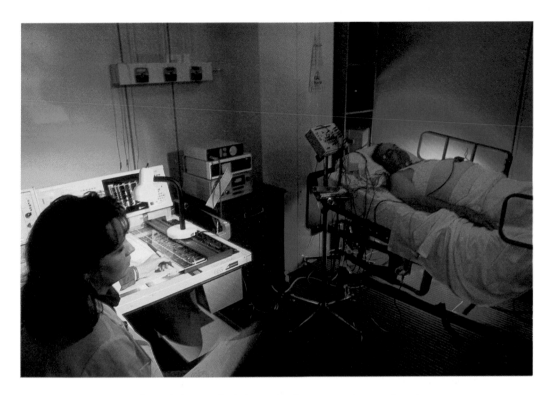

In a sleep lab a technician monitors a patient as he sleeps.

who have a much higher breast cancer rate. Such differences may be useful in predicting cancer risk and detecting early cases of breast cancer.

Another chronobiological study found that many newborn babies in families with a history of high blood pressure showed much greater circadian variations in blood pressure than babies from families without such a medical history. Monitoring of the blood pressure fluctuations of infants might be used as a general screening test. The families of babies found to be at risk could then be advised on diet and other measures to reduce the chances of the children developing heart disease.

✦ CAN WE TURN BACK THE AGING CLOCK? ✦

A number of popular books have made spectacular claims for melatonin, not only as a sleep regulator but also as a "miracle drug" that can strengthen people's defenses against disease, improve their sex life, and even make older people look and feel younger. The pineal gland plays a key role in helping to regulate the other endocrine glands and their hormones. In addition to keeping circadian rhythms synchronized with the day–night cycles, the pineal gland is important in sexual development. In many animals it sets the timing for seasonal mating cycles and signals the time to begin preparing for migration or hibernation.

U.S. medical researchers Walter Pierpaoli and William Regelson believe the pineal gland is the body's "aging clock." In a series of experiments on mice, they transplanted pineal glands from young mice into the brains of old ones and placed pineal glands from old mice inside the brains of young ones. The old mice with young pineal glands soon were looking younger and healthier and acting livelier than before the operation, and they lived an average of 30 percent longer than the normal mouse lifespan of twenty-four months. Kept under the same conditions and fed the same diet, the young mice that had been given old pineal glands quickly began showing signs of aging and died about 30 percent earlier than their normal lifespan. Giving "middle-aged" mice a daily dose of melatonin in their drinking water also had dramatic effects—they looked and acted younger than the controls (who received only plain water) and lived about six months longer than usual—a 25 percent increase. Many scientists are skeptical about whether these results on mice can be applied to humans, but many people are now taking melatonin each evening in an effort to stay young.

Is there an "aging clock" in the body that determines how long we will live? Scientists are not sure. The complete plans for development, both before birth and during childhood and adolescence, are coded in DNA, the chemicals of heredity, which make up the **genes** that are found in structures called **chromosomes** inside each body cell. But do the chromosomes also contain blueprints for the gradual breakdown of organs and systems that occurs as we grow old? Or is aging just the result of a series of mishaps from accidents, attacks by germs or harmful chemicals, and a general wearing out? Are there genes for staying young and healthy that are gradually turned off as we age? If so, scientists may someday learn to work the "switches" to turn these genes back on.

Leonard Hayflick, a researcher on aging, has established that there is a limit to how long normal body cells can go on growing and dividing. Some types of cells stop dividing early—by the time you were born, you had just about all the nerve cells and skeletal and heart-muscle cells you were ever going to get; if any were lost, they normally would not be replaced. Other cells, such as those in the skin and the lining of the mouth and nose, continue to divide all through life to provide replacements for ones that get worn out or damaged. When Hayflick tried to grow some of these cells in culture dishes, he found that cells from a human embryo were able to divide only about fifty times; then they started to die off. Cells taken from a child or an adult died after fewer divisions,

In early 1997 the world was stunned by the announcement that Scottish researchers had produced a **clone**—essentially an identical twin—from a cell taken from an adult sheep. Furious arguments raged about whether it was ethical to continue such experiments and whether anyone should ever try to make clones of humans. At the same time, there was a quieter debate among scientists about whether Dolly, the cloned lamb, would develop normally. A newborn animal conceived in the usual way develops from a brand-new cell, a fertilized egg; but Dolly started out her life as a set of chromosomes containing the hereditary information of a sheep who was already six years old. Would she start to age prematurely and live a shortened life? Those worries appear to have been groundless. Dolly not only grew into a healthy young sheep, but she mated and, the following spring, gave birth to a normal lamb of her own.

Dolly is a ewe whose fame comes from the fact that she was cloned from an adult sheep.

reflecting the fact that they had already divided a number of times since they were first formed. (For each type of cell, it takes up to about twenty cycles of cell division to produce an adult.) Many studies have confirmed the existence of this "Hayflick limit" to cell division. Cells from animals of other species have different limits, and the total number for each species is roughly proportional to the maximum lifespan of that kind of animal. But Hayflick points out that the limited number of cell divisions cannot really be the cause of aging, since most animals grow old and die long before the limit is reached. Some researchers are now looking for "longevity genes" that give animals stronger body defenses and permit them to live and stay healthy longer. Perhaps someday they can use a kind of gene therapy to help us to turn back our aging clocks.

GLOSSARY

axis—an imaginary line running through the earth from the North Pole to the South Pole.

biological clocks—built-in timing that regulates the rhythms of living organisms' bodies and activities.

biological rhythms—the timing of cycles of internal processes and behavioral activities of living organisms.

chromosomes—structures in the nuclei of cells that contain the genes, the hereditary information for the organism.

chronobiologist—a scientist who studies the internal rhythms of humans and other organisms.

circadian rhythms—cycles of activities or body processes that repeat at intervals of about one day (24 hours).

clone—a group of cells or organisms all possessing the same heredity; or an exact copy of an organism (identical twin) produced using the chromosomes from a body cell, not by sexual reproduction.

diurnal—active mainly during the daytime.

dormancy—a period of (relative) inactivity.

echolocation—a technique of locating objects by sending out sounds and interpreting the pattern of their reflections.

equator—an imaginary circle around the earth's middle, which is an equal distance from the two Poles.

equinox—the times of the year when the hours of daylight and darkness are equal: spring (vernal equinox) and fall (autumnal equinox).

free-running—the tendency of organisms to exhibit circadian rhythms even in the absence of external cues.

genes—instructions for making proteins, coded in a chemical called DNA; they are the chemical blueprints for traits that are passed on by heredity.

gravity—a force of attraction between two objects; the attractive force that holds objects to the earth's surface.

hibernation—a sleeplike state in which certain animals spend the winter.

hormones—chemicals secreted into the blood by endocrine glands that help to control and coordinate body activities.

hour—a unit of time representing 1/24 of the total cycle of daylight and darkness.

hypothalamus—a portion of the brain containing control centers for many body functions.

insomnia—an inability to fall asleep or to remain asleep for the normal time.

jet lag—a temporary disruption of the body's circadian rhythms due to a rapid change in time zones.

lunar—pertaining to the moon.

lunar month—the time it takes for the moon to revolve around the earth.

melatonin—a hormone secreted by the pineal gland that produces sleepiness and helps to regulate biological rhythms and reproductive cycles.

menses—the periodic flow of blood from the lining of a woman's uterus.

migration—periodic travels from one home to another to obtain better feeding or breeding conditions than a single habitat could provide.

nocturnal—active mainly during the nighttime.

pheromones—hormonelike chemicals that influence the behavior or body functions of other members of the same species.

photosynthesis—the production of food from simple chemicals (carbon dioxide and water) by plants and certain bacteria, using the energy of sunlight.

pineal gland—a gland deep within the brain that secretes the hormone melatonin.

premenstrual syndrome (PMS)—a complex of emotional and physiological disturbances that some women experience just before or during menstruation.

revolution—the movement of one body around another in a round or oval path called an orbit.

rotation—turning around an axis.

seasonal affective disorder (SAD)—a cyclic depression that occurs during the winter, when days are short.

solar day—the time it takes for the earth to rotate on its axis.

solar year—the time it takes for a complete revolution of the earth around the sun.

solstice—the times of the greatest difference between the hours of daylight and darkness. In the Northern Hemisphere the "day" is longest at the summer solstice and shortest at the winter solstice.

sundial—a device for measuring the passage of time according to the length of a shadow cast by the sun.

suprachiasmatic nucleus (SCN)—a control center in the hypothalamus that acts as one of the internal biological clocks.

tides—the periodic rises and falls of the water level in the ocean and certain rivers, due to the gravitational attraction of the moon.

ultradian rhythms—biological cycles that occur more than once a day.

zenith—the highest point, as of the sun in its apparent movement in the sky.

FURTHER READING

Austad, Steven N. *Why We Age: What Science Is Discovering about the Body's Journey Through Life.* New York: Wiley, 1997.

Coleman, Richard M. *Wide Awake at 3:00 A.M. By Choice or by Chance?* New York: W. H. Freeman and Company, 1986.

Dotto, Lydia. *Losing Sleep: How Your Sleeping Habits Affect Your Life.* New York: Morrow, 1990.

Gittelson, Bernard. *Biorhythm.* New York: Warner, 1980.

Hayflick, Leonard. *How and Why We Age.* New York: Ballantine, 1994.

Hughes, Martin. *Body Clock: The Effects of Time on Human Health.* New York: Facts On File, 1989.

Orlock, Carol. *Inner Time: The Science of Body Clocks and What Makes Us Tick.* New York: Carol Publishing Group, 1993.

Perry, Susan, and Jim Dawson. *The Secrets Our Body Clocks Reveal.* New York: Rawson Associates, 1988.

Pierpaoli, Walter, and William Regelson. *The Melatonin Miracle.* New York: Simon & Schuster, 1995.

Riedman, Sarah. *Biological Clocks.* New York: Thomas Y. Crowell, 1982.

Time-Life Student Library: Planet Earth. Alexandria, Virginia: Time-Life Books, 1997.

INTERNET RESOURCES

http://ericir.syr.edu/Projects/Newton/14/clocks10.html "Newton's Apple: Teacher's Guides: How do clocks keep time?" (information, resources, and activities)

http://physics.nist.gov/GenInt/Time/ancient.html "A Walk Through Time" (including Ancient Calendars, Early Clocks, Revolution in Timekeeping, The "Atomic Age," World Time Scales, and NIST Time Calibration)

http://www.brandeis.edu/new/fly2.html "Biological clocks no longer found only in the brain" (description of an experiment on flies)

http://www.cbt.virginia.edu/tutorial/HUMANCLOCK.html "The Human Clock..." (with additional pages on Historical Background, The Sleep-Wake Cycle, Shift Work, Transportation Accidents, Doctors' Hours and other medical applications, The Clock in Other Organisms, Other Rhythms: Infradian and Ultradian, and a glossary)

http://www.chronotherapy.com/ "What Makes You Tick?" (medical applications of circadian rhythms, including allergies, heart attacks, hypertension, matching drug therapy to the body clock, and "A Day in the Life of Your Body")

http://www.circadian.com/biological_clock.htm "Circadian Rhythms and Your Biological Clock" (a tutorial and "Owl and Lark Test")

http://www.sunnexbiotech.com/biological.html "Biological Rhythms and the Body Clock—the Basis of Light Therapy"

INDEX

Page numbers in *italics* refer to illustrations.